EH UP!

POETRY FROM YORKSHIRE

by

PETER J. WATSON

EH UP!
Poetry from Yorkshire
by Peter J. Watson

Copyright © 2025 Peter J. Watson

First published in Great Britain in 2025
by Wordbotherers Press
Scarborough, North Yorkshire

ISBN: 978-1-0684310-1-2

British Library Cataloguing in Publication Data.
A catalogue record for this book is available from the British Library.

Edited and designed by Dr Simon Robinson
Cover and interior illustrations by the author.

Typeset in Dancing Script, EB Garamond, Gentium Plus and Zeyada
Printed and bound by IngramSpark

For more information visit: www.wordbotherers.com

This is a work of poetry and creative memoir. Any resemblance to real persons, living or dead, is purely coincidental unless otherwise stated.

WORDBOTHERERS PRESS
SCARBOROUGH
MMXXV

WB
GROUP OF AUTHORS

"Finding the extraordinary in the ordinary."

"Raw, honest and relatable."

"Bittersweet."

"Proper Yorkshire."

Peter J. Watson (P.J.)

Poet. Observer. Yorkshireman. P.J. doesn't set out to impress —
he writes because life won't let him keep quiet. For him, poetry
is part therapy, part wrestling match: each poem gnawed at and
puzzled over until it finally agrees to sit on the page. Drawing
on years of watching people, places and peculiarities, he
captures everyday moments with honesty, warmth and a
sideways grin. There's humour in the ordinary, bruises beneath
the surface, and an unflinching eye for the daftness of it all.
A founder member of the Wordbotherers collective, P.J. shares
his work among fellow scribblers who know the satisfaction
(and torment) of getting words to behave. If you ask him for his
biography, he'll likely shrug. Everything you need to know is in
his poems.

Other Collections.

Poems from the Darkside
The Thistle and the Rose
Daftness and other afflictions

www.wordbotherers.com

INTRODUCTION

To read Peter J. Watson is to sit by a warm fire on a cold day, swapping tales with a friend who knows the world's rough edges and its rare moments of grace. These are poems that speak, as he puts it, from "deep within"—rolling around in the head until, at last, they tumble out and find their place on the page. They do not flinch from sorrow, nor do they pretend that joy is simple. Here you will find laughter and tears living in the same stanza, with daftness and pain held together in a quiet handshake.

Peter's words are forged from a life of ordinary wonders and extraordinary losses. He writes, "You never get over the loss of a loved one ... You learn to live with the loss and rebuild your life." That spirit of resilience—of moving forward "one step, and one day at a time"—echoes through these pages. There are poems for family, for friends, for the ones we have lost and the memories we hold close. There are poems for those invisible days, and for the ones when the world feels raw and funny and full of surprise.

You'll meet Yorkshire folk and enchanted puddings, old friends and vanished loves. There are moments of dark humour, of gentle mischief, and, running beneath it all, a sense that, however sharp life's griefs may be, "there is a way out." Peter's poems do not promise answers, but they offer a hand to hold on the journey.

So: pick up a cup of tea, take your time. These are words "out on loan"—and, for a little while, they are yours to keep.

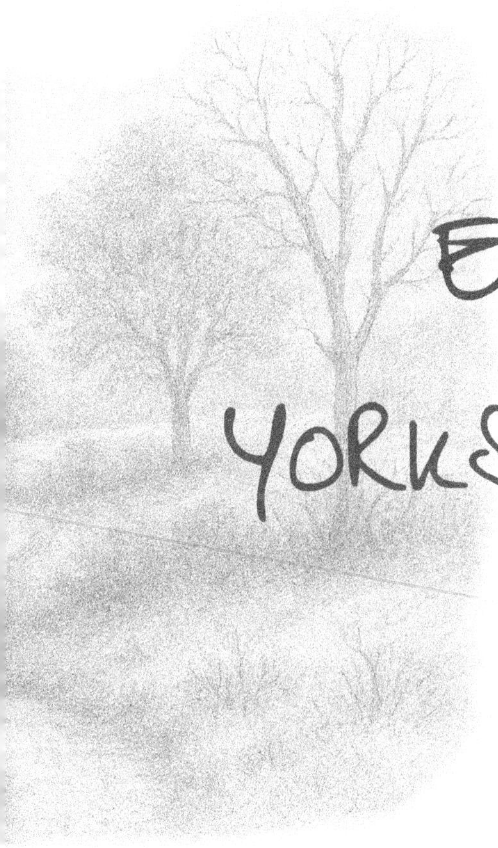

EH UP, YORKSHIRE!

YORKSHIRE FOLK

I never enjoy being enjoyable
It seems too much effort to me
I'd much rather sit watching telly
Alone with a big pot of tea

Maybe it's 'cos I'm from Yorkshire
We're known to be *miserable gets*
My friend who comes from Newcastle
Says, there's really no hope for you, *pet*

We're taught from being young children
Never ever to crack a small smile
If you do they say you're not normal
Then run from you, mile after mile

When we go out, our drink is *Best Bitter*
No Lager or Whiskey for us
You can make a pint last forever
Which of course, is for us such a plus

Our favourite food is *Yorkshire pudding*
Battered, plain, served with gravy or sweet
The more Yorkshire pudding you manage
We'll make sure, on your plate, there's more meat

I love that I come from *North Yorkshire*
Men are men, and women the boss
I married a woman from *Scotland*
To Yorkshire girls, not such a great loss

They think that up north of the border
That in Scotland they're miserable sods
Just try coming down into Yorkshire
We'll show you we're miseries Gods

Remember when you visit Yorkshire
Bring cash, *nowt-* here is given for free
You can have all the fresh air and views
But we'll charge you for *Yorkshire cream teas*

Make sure you don't come here too often
You might get infected and stay
We don't really want any more people
We wish you would all go away

It's hard sometimes living in Yorkshire
It's filling up, with many strange folk
They drink *G & T* on the terrace
Say '*cor blimey,*' and laugh at in jokes

It's important if you move to Yorkshire
Heed advice that I gave to my son
Never ever to show your true feelings
Except to those ones that you love

Then only together in private
Don't ever let people forget
Reputations important in Yorkshire
Pass it on, we're all *miserable gets*

We're not really stupid in Yorkshire
Just ordinary, plain - speaking folk
You see when you live in *God's country*
The rest of the world is *the joke*

We really enjoy being *miserable*
We're just Yorkshire folk and we're tough
We do have a great sense of humour
But, it's as *dry as like in the Sahara*
And *as daft as a worn - out old brush.*

PJ.
© 2019

The first line here is from an episode of Last of the Summer Wine.
Roy Clarke writes about a load of old men doing daft things
while the women watch them and shake their heads.
No one smiles and the most miserable character is called Smiler.
The women get all the best lines.
Yorkshire, and Yorkshire humour to a tee.

YORKIE BAR

Don't come to Yorkshire, it's a terrible place
Full of flat caps who get *reet* in yer face
It's cold and it's wet and dirty as hell
And the countryside's full of such god-awful smells
The people are dreadful and don't like strangers
If you disagree with their views
You are always in danger
The sea is polluted, the hotels are no good
The food is inedible, unless you like *Yorkshire pud*
It's better for all if you just stay away
Leave the Tykes in *God's country*
Offcomers don't enter and ruin our ways.

PJ.
© 2024

If you don't understand the irony of this poem,
you're not from Yorkshire.

T'POET

Another poet from Yorkshire
What's gone wrong with the bloody place
We're meant to be *dour* and *taciturn*
Not *emoting* all over the place

They've gone an made this un *t'laureate*
He says he don't care 'bout the money
Now listen lad tha's from Yorkshire
Saying stuff like that ain't bloody funny
Tha's been living too long down in *Oxford*
Too long it would seem amongst *spires*
Get *thissen* back home to Yorkshire
Have a pint and get lost in the mires
Tha'd best come home and help us
We're now wearing *Fedoras* not caps
The *whippets* have all disappeared
Everyone has bloody *cats*
Get *thissen* home, come and save us
Stop messing about with the Queen
What happened to that young *whippersnapper*
Who forever was our Gawain.*

PJ.
© 2021

*With sincere apologies to the UK's current Poet Laureate, Simon
Armitage C.B.E. A proper poet from Yorkshire.
He is now Professor of Poetry at the University of Leeds
(Yorkshire).
I suggest that you read some of his poetry.
* Simon Armitage wrote a modern version of Gawain and the
Green Knight*

Meet me in York

Meet me in St Louis
Okay then, York will do
I'm not such a romantic
I'm Yorkshire through and through

I'll never send you flowers
No long walks in pouring rain
I'm really a big *softie*
I just can't take the pain

I don't do big surprises
I'm scared no one will come
It's really very hard for me
To know you're my only one

It was never meant to happen
I'm just not built for this
I was never meant to meet you
My very special Miss

I'm never going to tell you
How much you mean to me
It's Yorkshire, *men don't do this*
Especially not me

I love you more than life
Just thought that you should know
I doubt I'll tell you this again
You'd better let it flow

I don't go in for romance
Life's not all hearts and flowers
I'm lucky that you found me girl
I'm so glad this love is ours

We'll never speak of this again
From now on you own my heart
Only death can come between us
Until then we'll never part.

PJ.
© 2019

*Yorkshire folk (men in particular) are not known for their
flamboyant gestures.
It doesn't mean that they don't love any less.
Of course, it may also be that if you are in a relationship with a
Yorkshire woman and if you bring her flowers or offer to take her
out her natural response is, "what have you done now?" or "what
do you want?"
Tricky!*

THA NO'S

I knew she was from Yorkshire
By the way she just said NO
If she'd been a Geordie
It might have been *haway* or
If she was from Scotland
It would certainly be *och nay*
Now, if she was from London
It might have been Ok

But as she was from Yorkshire
It was just a simple NO
She told me it would never happen
Not now, no bloody way
Come on now lad, just bide your time, you're going to have to wait
Don't get yer knickers in a twist
It's only our first date

PJ.
© 2024

Just in case any of you were wondering, this poem is about splitting the bill on a first date.

Nothing else.

Honestly!

HOME AND HEART

HOME

The Rye runs into the Derwent
The Derwent flows down to the sea
This land, these rivers, this Ryedale
These are the heart of me.
My life moves forward, and I move along
But Ryedale comes right along with me
This land holds my roots which are buried so deep
The fields and the moors sing my song
For all I have travelled, for all I have seen
This place is my home
This is where I belong

PJ.
© 2023

Self-explanatory really.

GRANDAD'S SHED

Grandads shed is a magical place
It's full of such *wondrous* things
We found some old soap, and cameras, green rope
Silver spoons in a blue leather box
Stuff he thought that he'd lost
All tied up and bundled with string

Thousands of nails in rusty old pails
With tools, set aside for the future
Things you never can find
When you need them, they hide
They can go on your rack, *you daft old pack rat*
You're sure to find use for them later!
Pots of old paint, that have rust on the top
Paint brushes too, all covered in goo
In jam jars, and even a tatty old mop
There are mugs by the dozen, a bright white bread oven
Inside it there was a *kazoo*
Some hosepipes and reels, a bike with no wheels
Cowboy boots, plastic bags by the pound
Everywhere that you look, something new to be found
Aladdin's cave where great treasures abound

We'll find Grandad in there with his eyes full of mist
But the look on his face is pure pleasure
Come on in he will cry, with a glint in his eye
I've found us some more *buried treasure*
Stuff I've had since a lad, look some rocks, they're not bad
I got them when caving in Cheshire

There are boxes with locks, no keys, but some socks
And some instruments to tell us the weather
There are some old soft toys, and games for small boys
Drum sets, vases, bright mirrors, whatever
You might need them again, is *Grandads refrain*
I think I will keep them forever

I mean to clean it all out, of that there's no doubt
But it's so hard to do don't you see
They're all memories to me, a *real family tree*
Of Grandma, and our lives together
I know what I need, more sheds, yes indeed
Let's go out and we'll buy some together

It's not just old crap, but a real treasure map
Grandads' life is there, measure for measure
These are not just bright things, to put in the bins
It's Grandads' life's work, that stupid old twerp
As he sits in his chair, a Stetson lies there
Who does he think that he is, *Wyatt Earp*

Not so daft as we think to hold on to these things
It's for us that he keeps all this treasure
They're his stories you see, that fill us with glee
Of his life and *our whole family*
So, tell us more tales, of all your travails
Say please, if you will, *our old fella*
Of the boxes you've found, on *this hallowed ground*

In your own special land, right there in your hand
The one that you call never, never
You become young again, in your shed there's no pain
Where your memories can live on forever.
You love it in there, in your *musty old chair*
Telling tales that keep us so rapt

Because we never knew, that you were young too
Making all of your plans, fell in love, holding hands
Without you we wouldn't be here
Then tell us old chap, before you have a nap
Of the *fun you and Gran had together*

It's not just the shed, they are *all in your head*
Those stories you tell
Write them down and we'll keep them forever
Then when we have our sheds, full of crap, so it's said
We can build, thanks to you, with our new crew
Our own little world, *our own special place*
That we shall all call never, never.

PJ.
© 2019

Every Grandad I know, or knew has a shed.
Some have more than one, some are big, some are small some are
just drawers or boxes. They have one thing in common. They are
ALL *full of crap. All the crap is stories waiting to be told.*
Things we can't bear to throw away, for whatever reasons they are
of great importance to us as Grandads.
Dads also have sheds. This is where it all starts.   Generally, with
the phrase; "I'll keep that, it might come in useful on day." Simple
as that.
They are then with you for life.
Nearly everything in my shed has a story.
My own collection has over the years, spilled into the house. I have
drawers full of stuff.
I am thinking of downsizing.
The new house **MUST** *have a shed, or maybe two!!!*

HITHER AND TETHER

Yan, Tan, Tether,
That's way *ti* count *tha* sheep
That's what *mi* Grandad *telt* me,
Afore I went *ti* sleep
Fasten *yat behint* the,
Tha musn't let 'em stray
Now; close thine eyes *mi* little un,
and *reest* amongst fresh hay
We've had a grand day, thee, and me
Thou running all hither 'n thither
Me trying to *kep* up *wid t'awd* dog
As we *chassed* them gimmers through *t'heather*
So. *Mek* sure that thee gets a good *reest*
'Cos tomorrow we're back out *ont brow*
When we'll *chass* 'em agin,
'til they're all *in't reet* pen
And I'll *larn* thee *ti* count *Shepherds measure.*

PJ.
© 2022

I spent a great deal of time with my Grandad when I was a child growing up in North Yorkshire.
He spoke in a dialect, specific to the area that has unfortunately long since gone.
I have tried to recapture, at least, the flavour of the language here.
And, of course the love we had for each other.

MEAT PIES, SCARVES & BOVRIL

(It's a funny old game)

Meat pies, scarves, and Bovril
Standing in the crowd
Football in the *seventies*
Women not allowed
Travelling with our team
In our special pack
Find the opposition
Go on the attack

Football in the *eighties*
Lots of tears about
Stadiums come crashing down
Blame it on the louts
It's now, about the bums on seats
Making football safer
Banning songs and sponsored shirts
The future's looking bleaker

Football in the *nineties*
Now it's Premier
Teams are reaching for the Sky
Chasing rarefied air
Clubs are full of players
Hola, Monsieur, Mon frère
Money buys you everything
The fans don't really care

Football in *two thousand*
It's all about the league
Not those little local ones
Europe. Yes, indeed
Women playing football
For professional clubs
If you take the time to watch them
They are really very good

Football now in *twenty-ten*
It's all about the owners
If you are an oligarch
Please come and take us over
Managers they come and go
Often at great speed
Spending owners millions
In their efforts to succeed

We're up to *twenty twenty*
Football has come far
It's up to speed, but slower
Since we all have VAR
We have so many pundits
Ex pros' waiting for the call
Let us please enjoy the game
We don't need you know it all's

Football is a *passion*
It's now on the TV all the time
I liked it best when it was pies
And swaying in long lines.
Football was for Saturdays
Radio results at five,
Then going out on Sunday
And playing *OUR game live.*

PJ.
© 2023

Yorkshire has a lot of football teams, and a lot of supporters. Pretty much without exception they all hate the Manchester clubs!!

YES DEAR

Yes dear, is the answer to all the questions that she asks
Yes dear, is the answer for all those little tasks
Yes dear, is the answer for most of all your life
Yes dear, is the answer if you want to please your wife
Yes dear, is the answer no matter what the question
Yes dear, is the answer to all of her directions
Yes dear, do you love me?
Yes dear, do you care?
Yes dear, what is wrong with you?
Why don't you ever share?
Yes dear, just two little words
That always mean so much
Yes dear; but you must mean them
Or she'll kick you into touch.

PJ.
© **2024**

A word of warning.
You will be asked an occasional rhetorical question and the answer
***MUST** be No dear.*
If you aren't paying attention, and give the wrong answer; that
my friends is where the fun starts.

LANDSCAPE AND MEMORY

SOFT VOICES

Flowing softly through the veiled birch grove
A stream cascades carelessly over the grey lichen covered rocks
Murmuring its lonely song, in a crystal- clear voice
Tumbling onwards, it falls into a translucent pool
Where the feral deer come to drink at dawn.
I fill my flask and quench my pain with the ice cold, invigorating
water
This purity elevates my spirit and dispels my anguish
I remove my jacket to use as a pillow
Lie back on the forgiving, untrammelled grass which drifts lazily
around the tree roots
Then I close my eyes.

I breathe deeply of the uncontaminated air and the intoxicating
silence
That are only to be found here
This magical place, untainted by humanity
A warm breeze gently *susurrates* through the tremulous leaves
Carrying the fragrance of the heather from the desolate moors that
enfold the grove
The quietude only broken by the mournful cry of my companion
A lone Curlew scouring the wilderness for its own lost love
I sense the embrace of the birch trees as they whisper to me in
their soft voices
You are home
You are home
You are home
You are with us now
Be at peace.

PJ.
© 2023

Yes, this place really does exist, high on the North York Moors.
I have been going there since I was a child.
Yes, I do feel at peace there
Yes, I feel not only at home there, but part of the landscape.
No, I am not telling you where it is.

SEASIDE

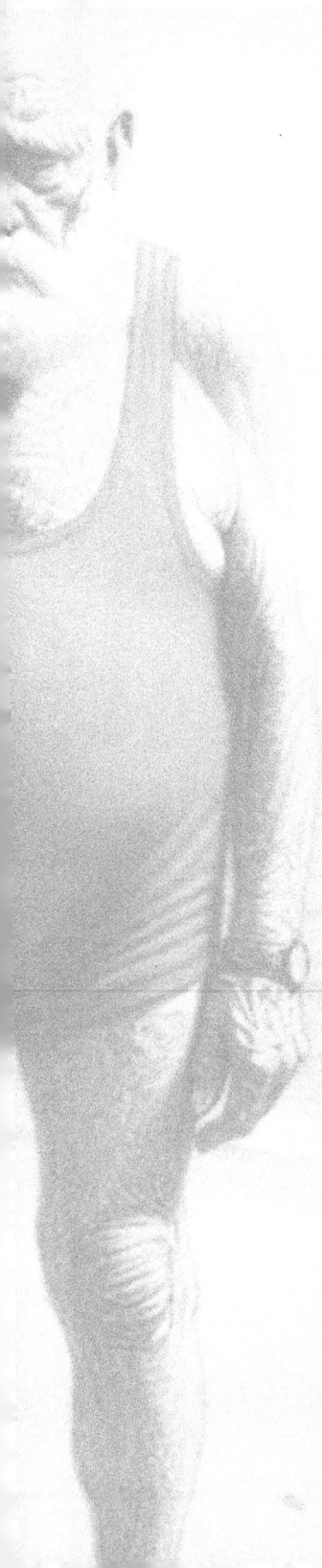

I took a body to the beach
I swear it was not mine
The costume, well, it used to fit
I should have taken that as a sign

I'd really worked so hard
To get myself in shape
Perhaps I really should not have had
That last slice of chocolate cake

Me toes are now all wrinkled
I've got sand right up me bum
Me face has gone *bright cherry red*
I look just like a *plum*

Me beach ball has deflated
Me sandcastle washed away
The seagulls nicked me fish and chips
Right from off me tray

Me deckchair has collapsed
Me windbreaks in the breeze
Me towel fell right off me back
When me trunks were at me knees

I lay down on me *sunbed*
To have a little sleep
The kids they covered me in sand
And now I've lost me teeth

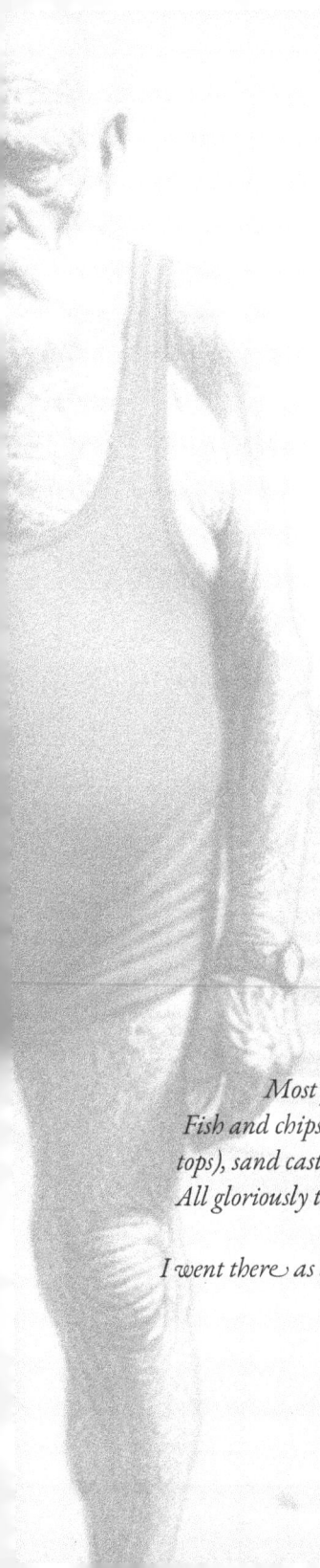

We'll go and get some candyfloss
And go onto the fair
A big ice cream along the front
And get us some fresh air

I really hate the seaside
But the grandkids shout and cheer
We've had a lovely week Grandad
Can we come back next year.

PJ.
© 2023

I really love the seaside.
Most particularly the Yorkshire coast.
Fish and chips eaten out of the paper, ice cream (yellow
tops), sand castles, theatres and amusement arcades.
All gloriously tacky, incredible fun yet steeped in history
and hardship.
I went there as a child, took my son there and I now go with
my grandson.

TACKING IN THE WIND

My life is changing course again
I'm tacking in the wind

The storm has blown out and gone
I'm looking for dry land
To find the safest harbour
I might just need a hand

The winds of change are blowing
Cruel and icy, fast and low
I'm tacking *'cos that's what I do*
There's nowhere I want to go

The wind that blew me on has gone
I need to find a way
I'm tacking in still waters
Got lost and gone astray

        In Yorkshire where I come from
        A child of my own kind
        When we were lost and listless
        They'd tell us to breathe deeply
        Relax and just unwind

                I need to 'tak a deep breath
                Like when I was a child
                And 'tak some wind inside me
                To generate my own storm
                Sail on to waters wild

If I don't keep on moving
Cutting through the waves
I'll tack alone forever
Just drifting to my grave.

PJ.
© 2018

This poem is about assessing your position after an
intense period of grief.

HELMSLEY MARKET DAY (MID-1960S)

Helmsley at the time that this memoir is set was the hub of the local farming community and there were still several working farms scattered within its boundaries. It was a less 'refined' town than it is now and was very much a rural, and thriving, market town of it's time. A wonderful place to grow up in. You knew most, if not all the people in the town, and they knew you which was fantastic if at times a little restrictive.

Friday was Market Day (still is), and the town came alive with market stalls erected to a specific pattern which never varied. This complex jigsaw of stalls was completed by the council workers, a hardy bunch of men identifiable by the Donkey Jackets they all wore to protect them from the weather. They worked long hours in all weathers though the local hill farmers thought they had it 'soft,' which of course these hard- working men did compared to the rigours of the small farmer. Setting up of the stalls had to be finished long before the official opening time of the market at eight am.

The traders needed to have their stall set out early to catch the older matriarchs, mostly widows or spinsters of this parish all dressed invariably in black, carrying wicker baskets, their hair pulled back into a tight bun underneath the best Friday bonnet, they looked like they had come straight out of a Charles Dickens novel. They always came early to market, come rain or shine, to find the freshest produce, at the best price. Grim faced, striding purposefully between each stall their high tightly laced black boots clicking on the tarmac, setting the rhythm of the opening market They always haggled with the traders, who knew them all and had probably set their prices a little higher so they could be talked down and everyone could go away happy, and come back next week for the game to start again.

Grandad, an inveterate early riser from years as a dairy farmer, used to take me along to the square to watch the hustle and bustle of the opening market. Everybody seemed to know him and he loved to catch up on all the gossip. Many of the matriarchs used to come over for a quick natter. Grandad had recently become a widower and they all came to ask how he was coping. These stony-faced somewhat intimidating women had warm hearts and kind eyes once you looked beyond the face they showed the world, no doubt to hide their own pain.

You don't show your emotions in Yorkshire.

They always had a kind word for 't'little lad,' and sometimes even a goodie or two would appear from the voluminous black dresses they wore. Of course, this attention given to us wasn't all altruistic. These women loved a good gossip and Grandad was the hot topic at present, having recently become a widower. They were the 'newshounds' of the town and always had something of interest to say about some worthy of the local populace, as long as we understood that we didn't hear it from them.

There was one trader who fascinated me. He came from the mysterious land that was the West Riding of Yorkshire. Grandad and I loved to watch him in action. He sold everything from dinner services to swathes of cloth, all at "knock down prices" gathering a crowd around his stall with his patter recited in the language of that part of the county. We all came from Yorkshire, but his accent was totally different to ours. Emanating from the area somewhere around Leeds his vowels were flatter than ours and sounded harsh to my ears. The area we lived in retained many words of old Norse as part of the local dialect, held over from our Viking origins in this part of this vast county.

"Th'all not believe what ahs deeing tiday Missus. Ahm not selling, ahs gieing stuff away" and off he went. "T'missus el kill me when I get yam, nah then lass, how de yer fancy this little tea caddy alt way fra India, special today. Not at ten bob, not at five bob nobbut hef a crown. Ahl even throw in this measuring spoon for free for fust ten customers. Nah then, form an orderly queue, ladies." Even the hard, stony -faced matriarchs were putty in his hand. Often giggling like schoolgirls at his sometimes-fruity banter. They parted with their hard-earned money with smiles on their faces and never haggled about the price. The man was a true artist.

Most of the traders though came from within a thirty mile or so radius of the town and had been coming to ply their wares for years. There was a hard core of regulars the fish man from Scarborough, and his 'fresh fish' always sold out early and was often gone by noon.

My favourite was the sweetie stall, run by a man of extreme girth and a smiling face who gave the impression that he literally ate into his profit margin. It was absolutely packed with jars full of an enormous variety of goodies to tempt the kids and those with a sweet tooth. Once you had made your selection these were carefully weighed out in the enormous scales and poured reverently into brown paper bags. He took your money with a big smile and told you not to eat them all at once. Probably didn't mean it. It was his business after all, to provide the kids with the requisite amount of E Numbers and sugar, so the local dentist could remain in gainful employment. Grandad always bought me a 'mixed bag' and swore me to secrecy as Mum probably wouldn't approve.

The market was much more important than just a bargain hunters paradise (although, you could buy anything from a cauliflower to crockery.) It was a social occasion. If you sat on the steps that surround the Feversham Memorial for long enough you were almost certain to see everyone in town.

By nine am, most of the 'matriarchs' had gone home and the market was ready for the next wave of customers.

The farmers from the wild country that surrounded the town descended 'en masse' on a Friday to buy their supplies for the week and to catch up on all the local gossip. They rarely saw anybody except their own families during the week, carving out a hard livelihood on their small farms. Little patches of green, bounded by dry stone walls, keeping the wild at bay, scattered amongst the heather of the high ground. Hardly any of the farms had mains electricity, inside plumbing or a public water supply, and none had telephones. It was a hard life and they looked forward to the break from their unremitting slog that Market Day brought. They arrived in a wide variety of vehicles ranging from beaten up, barely legal vans and ex-army land rovers, to horse and carts. Most came with their wives and associated pre-school children, and of course the obligatory sheep dog. It was a fabulous, entertaining riot of noise and colour. The highlight of the week.

By eleven o'clock most of the farmers had completed their business with the market traders and for them, the real business of the day was about to start. Licensing laws were far stricter in the sixties than they are now but market days were an exception and the pubs were open from eleven am to eleven pm. The farmers had packed their purchases in their chosen method of transport, sent the wife and kids off to visit friends or family in the town, but kept their dogs with them and got down to the serious business of the day, always conducted in the pub.

It was great fun watching these normally dour gentlemen staggering, with great concentration from pub to pub, trying to fill their pipes with the black twist they all seemed to smoke, whilst at the same time keeping a watchful eye out for 'the Missus' who might have the temerity to drag them away from an important business meeting in one of the four pubs that surrounded the market square. These meetings were normally conducted of course, over frothing pints of *Best Yorkshire Bitter.*

Grandad took me home for lunch where I was left with my aunt, one of the aforementioned hill farmers' wives on her Friday visit, before making his way back to the market "to do a bit of business" for himself.

By 5pm the market was gone, packed away until next Friday. Of course, the pubs were still open, and generally packed out. *But that is another story for another day.*

It was the only day that anything exciting happened in the town.

Market day still exists in Helmsley, although the market itself is much smaller now. Many of the characters that ran the stalls are long gone. So too have the small farmers and their somewhat reckless consumption of beer. The market and the town are much less colourful without them.

But as I said, Helmsley and its market are much more refined than they used to be.

PJ.

MYTH, MISCHIEF & THE MARVELLOUS

THE ENCHANTED PUDDINGS

(A Modern Fairy Tale)

There is a myth in a small town in North Yorkshire, that many years ago a wild Haggis was captured by a Yorkshire Pudding.

It is a story so fantastic that many people still find this hard to believe, even now.

There are good reasons for this.

The true Haggis lives in the highlands of Scotland and rarely leaves its homeland. It is a very difficult creature to see as it is extremely shy, blends in with its surroundings and often wears different tartans as camouflage. Very few people ever get to see a true Haggis, and even less people understand their nature. Secretive and thick skinned they can be fierce if approached without care. It is these attributes that make the Haggis almost impossible to capture, and once caught difficult to keep in captivity, unless of course, they choose to stay.

These though are protective measures, as the Haggis has a tender heart.

Unlike the Haggis, Yorkshire puddings are not rare. In fact, they are plentiful around the world. However, proper Yorkshire puddings are still hard to find.
Made from unassuming ingredients, everyone thinks that they are simple, and uncomplicated. Not true. If handled badly they can be hard and sour, or limp and tasteless. Being from Yorkshire they always know what's best, and of course are never wrong. Not unlike the Haggis.

It is one of life's great mysteries that although never fully tamed that this Haggis chose to spend the rest of its life with this Yorkshire Pudding.
The main questions that are raised here are: What was the Haggis doing so far away from home? How did a plain and simple Yorkshire Pudding manage to capture such a magical creature? And why did the Haggis choose to spend its life with the Yorkshire Pudding?
For a plain Yorkshire pudding to capture a wild Haggis, well, let us just say it got lucky and leave it at that.
I personally think that the Haggis allowed the Pudding to capture it, BUT then let the Pudding think that it was clever enough to catch it.

Tricksy creatures these Haggi.

This is their story:

There was a Yorkshire pudding
Sad and lonely on the plate
It stared around, tears in its eyes
Then saw a vision at the gate

What kind of creature are you?
The pudding asked bare faced
I'm from a foreign land it said
The Chieftain of our race

The pudding said: It's Yorkshire
We are the masters here
You were it said, your fates just changed
Now let me make that clear

I am a creature of the North
Where we run wild and free
I came to this strange place by chance
How can YOU see the real me

That's easy cried the pudding
You have a special glow
That thick skin that you wear outside
Is really a disguise. I know!

You're soft and gentle inside
You're peppery and sharp
But most of all fierce creature
You have a *gentle heart*

What is your name? The pudding asked
Haggis the vision spoke
I have this recipe to share
That only you and I will ever know

The Haggis whispered to the Pud
A message from its heart
Only you can call me *Trish* it said
From now on, *we'll never part*

The Pudding was enchanted
Not lost now, not alone
For in this wild exciting girl
This Pud had found his home

So off they flew together
These puddings both grew wings
To have their great adventures
That only true love brings

They spent their lives together
This Haggis and this Pud
The glow that did surround them
Was their *recipe of love*

The moral of this story
Is right there at the start
When you are lost and all alone
True love will appear and steal your heart

So always love your puddings
At the end or at the start
With gravy, custard, or ice cream
They're always the best part

You might just find your special one
To feed you when it's dark
But heed this warning carefully
They'll always break your heart

The plain truth, as improbable as it sounds, is that this is no myth,
it is, in fact a true story.
I know this with absolute certainty because I am that Yorkshire
pudding, and I did indeed capture my Haggis.
The price I paid for capturing my Haggis was a high one. She said
she would stay with me for life, but I had to promise to give her my
heart and my soul in return.
In the end I gave them freely to spend my life with this magical,
but dangerous and unpredictable creature. I never regretted my
decision for one minute.
After nearly fifty years together, and many fabulous adventures
my Haggis had to leave me. She didn't want to go, but there was a
flaw in the mix that poisoned my Haggis, and she faded away.
She has now returned home to run free in the Highlands of
Scotland that she loved and where she belongs.
This Yorkshire Pudding is once again sad and lonely on the plate,
just a soggy mess without my Haggis at my side.
I do know though that I will run with my Haggis again when she
calls for me, as she will in time
We will spend eternity together, running wild and free like we
used to do.

Enchanted by each other, as was our fate.

PJ.
© 2019

Well: that's the myth.

Is this a true story of enduring love?

I'll let you decide!

WEREWOLVES OF BEMPTON

There is a quaint little town in North Yorkshire
Called Bempton. It's right by the sea
It's famous for its cliffs and wild birds
And this seemed quite attractive to me

So, I took myself off for a visit
Bought a ticket and got on the bus
Had myself a nice stroll on the cliff
Looked at birds, and didn't cause a fuss

As I was buying some scones for my dinner
The local shopkeeper whispered to me
It's a full moon tonight, just be careful
Bempton's full of Werewolves you see

I went to look for a pub, and a drink
Not only to settle my nerves
But I wanted to see if her story was true
It really did sound quite absurd

I found one. Its sign was the Wolfs Head
A pentangle hung over the door
As I entered, I couldn't help notice
There were scratch marks all over the floor

I went up to ask the Inn keeper
Who had a great whiskery jaw
His hands were huge, dark, and hairy.
His long fingernails, looked just like claws

Pray tell me good sir, could I have a pint?
And what is that pentangle for?
He gave me a look that said, careful
And his eyes they started to glow

It would be better for you, my young man
If you never should have to know
Now you go and sit at that table
You're just in time for our show

I went and sat down at the table
But kept my eyes fixed on the door
It was then that I spied a dark beauty
A wild local, that was for sure

She came and she sat down beside me
And said, would you like to talk
It will be a full moon much later
Perhaps, we could go for a walk

I thought with some trepidation
That I might just give this one a miss
It was then that she pounced, out of nowhere
And gave me a wondrous kiss

I went for that walk in the moonlight
With that girl, who now is my wife
She may NOT be a werewolf from Bempton
But by God we've a wonderful life.

So, remember, if you visit Bempton
And you think you hear howls at the moon
It's Karaoke on Sunday down the Wolfs Head
We're there, singing along, out of tune

Of course, there's no werewolves in Bempton
As a local I now know this to be right.
Although I arrived as a vegan
It is just a strange quirk of my life
That I now have a taste for raw meat off the bone
Wild camping, and running at night.

PJ.

I was at a friend's house in Bridlington, (Bempton is just up the coast). We were celebrating new year rather enthusiastically. One friend was 'having a rest' on the sofa when she suddenly sat bolt upright and exclaimed "There's Werewolves in Bempton you know'. Then promptly lay back down again. I was crying with laughter. So, I did some research later.
N.B. Bempton cliffs are well known to ornithologists, and well worth a visit.

PAM AND VERA

Polythene Pam and Vinyl Vera
Two old birds from a different era
Pretty young things from the age of punk
Brassy and sassy and permanently drunk
Grey haired now, and in a permanent funk

Swore they'd live very different lives
Yet both ended up as suburban housewives
They meet every Tuesday with Steradent Stan
Then drive into town in the back of his van

Living it large, in their torn black jeans
Varicose veins glinting through the seams
Safety pins, and black mascara
Mingled with wrinkles to create a farrago

They holiday at Butlins 70's weekenders
Inclusive of drinks and go on benders
Dance the pogo and pose and pout
Wearing surgical stockings 'cos they both have gout

No one from the Institute would ever guess
Just what they wear underneath their Sunday best
Crotchless knickers and a man's string vest
In case they both get lucky they are ready to impress

Polythene Pam and Vinyl Vera
Two old birds from a different era
They frequent all their favourite dives
But are home by ten to their mundane lives
They never forget that they are punks
Still living it large in a permanent funk

PJ.
© 2024

Pam and Vera are by no means exclusive to
Yorkshire, although it is their natural habitat.
They can be found throughout the world, generally
haranguing people from their mobility scooters.
Keep an eye out for them!

P'TERRY NEEDS T'PEE

Pterry the pterodactyl
Was having a pterrible time
He pthought he needed a p
He'd held it a very long time

Pterry was ptruly pterrified
And pthought it would last forever
Until T'Poet from Yorkshire said
It was only a ptyping error.

PJ. © **2024**

With its silent P a Pterodactyl sounds like it comes from Yorkshire.
Written for my Grandson.

A final word...

If you've enjoyed these little ramblings, you'll find more of Peter's works — and plenty more besides — with the Wordbotherers over at:

www.wordbotherers.com

Go on, have a nosey. We don't bite.